GUT FEELING

Lucy Hurst is a poet and writer, with a PhD in creative writing from York St John University. Her work often discusses chronic illness and disability through experimental forms. Her first pamphlet, *Modern Medicine*, was published by Fly on the Wall in 2021, and its title poem was shortlisted for the 2020 Bridport Prize.

Also by Lucy Hurst

Modern Medicine   (Fly on the Wall Press, 2021)

CONTENTS

HIGH RISK / HIGH REWARD   7

GAG REFLEX   9

ASTRAL PROJECTION   10

GUT FEELING   11

USED TO IT   15

INDIGESTIBLE   16

KNOW THYSELF   17

EXTREMELY CLINICALLY VULNERABLE   18

HARD TIMES   27

AFFORDABLE THERAPY   28

THE BED   30

SQUARE BREATHING   31

ACID REFLUX   32

ANIMAL INSTINCT   35

EVERYTHING IS BLUE   36

THE MAP   38

THE GUTS I HAVE LEFT   39

TINY WORLD   47

INNER BABY WORK   48

VITALS   49

ON BEING CONTAGIOUS   50

SELF-SURGERY   56

AN EROTIC POEM FOR VAMPIRES   59

ACKNOWLEDGEMENTS   63

ISBN: 978-1-917617-23-9

Cover designed by Aaron Kent

Cover image: © phive2015 / Adobe Stock

Edited by Kit Ingram

Typeset by Aaron Kent

Broken Sleep Books Ltd
PO BOX 102
Llandysul
SA44 9BG

Gut Feeling

Lucy Hurst

Broken Sleep Books

HIGH RISK / HIGH REWARD

I leave my phone at home
for the first time in a month
& let my emails go unread
pretending I haven't noticed
them yet

a gust warps the shape
of my breathing
casting it into an endless flow
I negotiate my way through flesh—
the tree's contorting spine

by the lake
insatiable ripples suckled
by spider   by fly
guttural bacteria bubbling up
as reactionary to this world

crashing inside & out
my body-mind cracking open like an egg
spewing into a body-on-body continuity
I pour out the anxiety in my head
into the fresh air

latest tinder bio: 'high risk, high reward'
'risk' now given second meaning
once   of my perceived perils
of dating as a sick person
& twice being truly *high-risk*

I correct the degrading comments
that seep into my line of thinking
standing under the bathroom light
no longer as corrosive
but softer   softer

GAG REFLEX

when I think of all the hands on & in my body
I find myself hard-pressed for the unscathed—
my secrets bare in a handful of x-ray images
a reflex to recite my name & date of birth
& a muscle memory so raw that examinations
feel like they're still happening after the fact
I get into position before the doctor finishes
speaking before he presses his palm into
my abdomen before the stethoscope checks
four points on my back & two on my front
it takes a camera being piped down my throat
for me to hit a limit of what I want to know
by now I've seen my entire digestive tract
lit up on a TV as I choked down my tears
I feel like they are looking for something
that's not there—a set of keys that had fallen
in gaps between my ribs or something
much smaller   a figurine   a russian doll
I'm so full of myself & so acutely aware
of all this space I take up
the proximity of one limb to the next
sometimes I forget where I begin & end
my insides flipped out a body inverted
I am outpouring life from elsewhere—
biological therapy & IVs of potassium
pounds & pounds of bacteria   vaccines
synthetic oestrogen   a flexi-camera
iced coffee   tall glass of water   gas & air
the doctor tells me it's easy I can take it
I open my body's borders *mind over matter*

ASTRAL PROJECTION

there are very few ways
to take respite from yourself
I do it quietly, economically
asphyxiation of my nervous system
memory in a chokehold
one pain management technique
suggests pretending it isn't happening
gaslighting your nerves to oblivion
& hyper-fixating on numbness
till it swallows you whole
it'll work   for a while
in my bouts of disassociation
I imagine leaving my body behind
I tell my friends in good humour
'I've not gone far,
just down here'
I avoid saying the obvious Ifindmybodyuninhabitable
IthinkIamdyingwithinmyself
when I lose a quarter pint of blood in diarrhoea
a nurse asks, *does this happen every time?*
my body's a touchy subject
an open-ended wound
I deliberate over pressing the button
imagining a digital notice board above the bed
watch me ugly cry for a paracetamol
I didn't know how much I was hurting
when I was released
& that pain repressed gnaws its way
through every version of the self
killing the entire zodiac sun moon & rising

GUT FEELING

The gastrointestinal tract has 100 million nerve cells in two
layers from the oesophagus to the rectum. It is called the 'enteric
nervous system'; it knows long before I or anyone else ever could.

I leave my brain indisposed & try to follow my gut
feeling. In the back of my mind, I skirt around the question—*what
is the difference between intuition & anxiety?* If deep down both
things co-exist, some part of me must be able to differentiate.

I try to feel without thinking—collapsing inwards into
that knowledge I know I have somewhere. As the heart knows
how to beat, as lungs know how to breathe.

One huge swollen nerve ending juts out like a promenade into the sea.

I have sat in this office, in this chair, in my mind, pretending I am above it—that I am the driving force behind my body, my intuition lay outside of my grasp. I run on overdrive.

It'll catch up on me—the messages it keeps sending—the morse code—the lightbulb that switches on.

I sense it all at my nerve endings. I feel it all from some place deeper. I know it all, only once it is too late.

When you dug inside of yourself, what did you find? I spiralled so far inward; I ended up on the outside.

Confronted by all the things my body knows but wouldn't let my mind in on till now. I start to cave.

I know a tenderness is required of me if I want to stop being as sick, if I want to feel my emotions in real-time. When I drink, I think about how a lighter click could burst me into flames.

How unbearable it must be to know everything. I refuse to see it; I can't bear to look.

cold saline
pushed through
a butterfly
in the nook
of my arm
hand or wrist
sharp scratch
to the vein
it tastes metallic
or it smells
metallic
& I'm thinking
that I can taste
it as it travels
through me
I feel it all over
as it seeps under
my skin
like bitter rain

USED TO IT

cracked back arched & legs open
spread eagle on the papered bench
obeying requests like commandments
a series of uncomfortably shaped tools—
I've become docile in ways I don't want
to be—
& the day never seems to come when
I get over the illness   the intrusion
my eyes grow sore as the realisation hits
that parts I thought had gone undisturbed
have been tested on before & everything
I want to keep sacred must withstand

INDIGESTIBLE

the doctor shows me my liver
& tells me it's where all my toxins are
in it I have grown a benign tumour
small enough to swallow.

I consider naming it, but nothing feels
suitable—I watch closely to see
if the toxic things I have collected
will grow like children.

KNOW THYSELF

if antibody levels can be tracked by monitoring
then I can transgress past the need to know anything
let my blood become the sum of my experience
& chalk these symptoms down to *who-knows-what*

I watch my dinner spit & boil over,
spinning in the soft glow of the microwave
imagining driving myself in for an M.O.T.
& letting a strong man do the heavy lifting
reducing my mood to a smiley face on a post-it
or tapping my head like fixing a TV antenna

I feel most alive when the disqualified realm
of what we don't know becomes insurmountable
when I look into the world   & it looks back
when the comedic timing collapses
& I catch the microwave:
00:01

The NHS has identified you, or the named person you care for, as someone at risk of severe illness if you catch Coronavirus (also known as COVID-19). This is because you have an underlying disease or health condition that means if you catch the virus, you are more likely to be admitted to hospital than others.

I have been sent fourteen letters
titled 'extremely clinically vulnerable'
they read:
>   where there are people there is risk
>   where there is proximity there is danger
>   where there is intimacy there is contagion

I'm told that I am ill & that
the threat of illness is everywhere
but how do I avoid what I can't see?
when there is no graph on the 5 o'clock news
did we ever find out whether we achieved
herd immunity in the end?

- minimise the time you spend with others in shared spaces (kitchen, bathroom & sitting areas) & keep shared spaces well-ventilated
- aim to keep 2 metres (3 steps) away from others & encourage them to sleep in a different bed where possible
- use separate towels &, if possible, use a separate bathroom from the rest of the household, or clean the bathroom after every use
- avoid using the kitchen when others are present, take meals back to your room to eat where possible, & ensure all kitchenware is cleaned thoroughly

at the dinner table I'm asked to pass the blame

there is more to go around than food

we talk about the utilitarian approach to ventilators

& which of us would be safe

none of us feels comfortable in asking—

who among us would define an expendable life?

This guidance applies to clinically extremely vulnerable individuals only. Others living in a household with someone who is clinically extremely vulnerable are not advised to follow this guidance.

when the doors close   the carriage
becomes a barrel of coughs
[gunshot sneeze] [round of wheezing]
& everyone looks fine   as in unphased
as in not thinking about it as in not panicking
as though nothing had ever happened
& everyone is playing one big joke
that I'm not in on

        I am the only person
        in this train carriage
        who is wearing a mask—
        & I start to feel
        self-conscious for it

                as if I am just
                paranoid
                as if none of it
                ever happened

it does involve greater risks for you as you will be increasing the number of people you have contact with.

what am I supposed to do if I
can't stop thinking about viruses
I'm full of the thought
in my lungs
in my veins
I find myself searching for
'jobs with good ventilation'
'subscription package for face masks'
'cafes and pubs with gardens'
'closest vaccination site'
'covid in your area'
I feel like I have been left behind—
for everyone else there is a before
& after
but I'm still waiting

We know that this is a difficult time & many people are making significant sacrifices. Thank you for your efforts to keep yourself & others safe.

anxiety is sickness. the root cause of sickness is sickness. *that thing that happened* to you was a sickness. it made sickness in you. violence is a sickness. pollution is a sickness. sickness is hard work. hard work causes sickness. medication for sickness causes sickness. medication for the medication is hard work. desperation is a sickness & hard work. no sleep is a sickness. too much sleep is a sign of sickness. self-psychoanalysis is hard work. overthinking is sickness. falling on *bad times* make sickness. man-made sickness. conspiracy theory sickness is just hard work. government-borne sickness. birth sickness. vomiting & viral sickness is hard work. body dysfunction is hard work. social body dysfunction is sickness.

AFFORDABLE THERAPY

when she died, I cried as if I knew her
& every time after in my floods of tears
I blamed it on my dead aunt
till at some point my mum intervened—
my brother does the same, but he blames the dog.
the vulnerable bit is already happening,
I am crying to a stranger again. In adulthood,
all my embarrassment became second-hand
as I detached from myself & checked in & out
of relationships till I found I was a common
denominator (maths was never a strong suit)
in my inner child work, my nervous system,
recalibrated like a DS with a chewed stylus
probably still in my blood metaphorically,
or accumulated in microplastics along with
the chewing gum blown in a permanent bubble
as to make a permanent gap—
Is this the best place to start?
I took the advice & ran with it putting obstacles
between myself & the feeling a CAHMS cup of tea
a shower   a long walk down a wet beach
but shame swells up swole & soon enough
I have forgotten which timeline I am in—
the feeling started when   no, it all started
when   no, there was no beginning there was just—
no, let me start again, please can we begin again?
my feelings became big & gross & hard to conceptualise
so, to save on the brainpower,

I decided I am the first person to ever feel shame,
or at least it feels that way—
next to a photo of myself, I have captioned
'I feel sorry for her, but not me,' I can't quite explain why—
I can't let myself down like this, I want to exist to myself,
I am trying to tell you all of this,
that the shame grows in the damp silence, the pause,
the parenthesis (where the gaps between the words
say the things I had hoped were not possible)

THE BED

a nurse presses two fingers into my wrist
looks down at her watch & clutches hard
enough to kickstart a pulse to calm her
I crack a joke & she jumps
at night partners admit to watching
to see if I'm passed out or passing away
I breathe gently & in the morning
I'll be galvanised by the 7 o'clock alarm
just to get up   & make my bed

SQUARE BREATHING

life falls as peripheral
slim fit in the corners of the eye
& in the centre   a black hole
my therapist asks me what it is
& what it feels like   not silky or matte
it is something to put your arms into
& it would wipe them clean off—
          it's not a lack of feeling
it's too much of the wrong thing
an active compression   the quashing
of the self   the restraint
it is being told not to feel
to keep quiet   to crush it
& under that great weight it buckles
emotion shattering—
how small I was
how small I was made to be
& as I stare into that blackness
colour draining
I look up into the mirror
& tell myself that I am loved
& I will go out & fucking act like it

as if someone has opened my
chest to look at my heart then
left it open minds as ours
tend to bend & break but all
the things I can't say in just
any tone of voice or the dangerous
thoughts I have crushed down will
all come out when I'm with you
because I believe it when you say
you can see me even when I can't
I have spent too much of my time
pretending to be unaffected by
these things saying they don't hurt
me but they do *they do   they do*
I'm trying to give myself patience
but it is hard to forgive myself—
all I want to know is how to forgive
the lump in my throat? the one
that chokes me every time the acid
gets high & my stomach can't
stomach it any longer when the
past finds new ways to come
back to us time & time again but
I don't want to leave the world
the way I entered it—crying &
bloody in the local hospital
I don't want to leave the world
the way I found it   because that
was never going to be good

enough I want to get out of it—
the loop of incessantly violent
hands I want us all to be out of
it   to do something productive
with all this emotion   not lose
humanity   or the ability to care
just because we have to pay
taxes I like to think that I'm
better than that I'm tired of news
reports of people having to beg for
care   in one way or another
I'm tired of acting like things
can only ever be one way forever
when you told me you felt it too
all I wanted to do was cry I know
just how much this can hurt   &
the thought that you feel it too
is next to unbearable—I wish I
could reach inside your mind
& pull out whatever demon is
hiding in there I wish I could
feel it for the both of us but I
can't I don't know how to we
have   both   felt   that   violence
in the hands of someone else but
it is not on yours or mine—on
your   palms I write out letters to
your nervous systems (whichever
needs to hear it the most) their
lines tell me you have life left
to live   & a heart   *o* such a heart

still pounding away I read it
all I want you to know that I would
have loved you before & I still do
the same—no event or bad thought
could make me think less of you &
I know making our own safety is-
exhausting but it is the only thing
that matters in times of crisis (which
is all of the time) it is much more
than walls it has heart it has soul &
it has rooms full of fresh air & heat
& fast Wi-Fi & a fridge with food in
it & only ever has soft voices
I know this illness kills us much
more than we would ever want to
admit to but if you pick up the
phone I'd remind you that
for you I'd use up my time
in minutes if it meant I could spend
them with you sat in parks
or cooking dinner on a weekday
as you jump on the train I catch
myself blowing a kiss like a friend
of mine did to me the week before
I hope it gets passed along up &
down the cross-country line I hope
this is the only infectious thing you
catch this year I would catch the
world & give it to you
if I could I would do anything—
if we can both feel the same thing
I hope you can feel this too

ANIMAL INSTINCT

under the fatal tenacity of the sun
heat becomes oppressive
infringing on reducing itself down

to a mere metaphor
I cease & tense as a balloon
lethargic on the ground

they say this inflammation
the inability to digest or retain food
acts as animalistic function

the removal of weight to
flee faster from predators—
my emotional extremities go cold

at the thought & as they warm & thaw
they grow a newfound sensitivity—
I wish I had known what it meant

a reaction called *abnormal*
it took me far too long to realise
that I should have listened

EVERYTHING IS BLUE

motion sick   laid on my back
watching as the sky reels a serial
of images
        duck
                duck
                        goose
      a heavy cloud

I feel nauseous in the migraine of flies
starting to feel gravity in new ways
that I can't explain   I'm in a mood
to advocate on behalf of my own devil
clutching onto his horns like pearls
pulling at each thought till their threads
come undone & meaning collapses—
I have been so many people that I start
to wonder which of them is really me
I try to explain that not everyone can find
words that feel *good enough*   some of us
are left at the fringe of language
but I don't want to be viewed under
this overhead lighting anymore
only underneath the sun

I try to define myself by what I am not
reaching for things outside of myself
raising my hands to try to touch the sky
just to find out I'm already in it

& all the tears I have cried in the span
of our phone call will make their way
back to me someday   as the rain
when I cry that I don't know who I am
or that I don't know what is going on
when I can't grasp at words   I know
I can grasp onto you—
you know me enough that the answer
no longer matters how lovely
it is to be seen through the eyes of
someone who loves you this much

now   whenever I introduce myself
to somebody new a friend of a friend
I have to invent a version that is palatable
someone who translates to language well
use a term that doesn't fit quite right
drawing a circle around myself
till the image of me comes through
when people ask about you
I don't know how to explain how I feel
when I miss you I just say:
the walls are blue
the curtains are blue
everything is blue

THE MAP
After Elizabeth Bishop

fingers run the map till they grow topographical

ink delineating the land from sea

muted green shadow hill sitting perched above

a once rarefied ultramarine now in synthetic abundance

as I press & mark the paper

I feel my hand becoming the sea

the skin an organ habitat of supple agility

my outward front reaching everything

I can taste the sun the sea the sulphur

permeating the page as it permeates me

THE GUTS I HAVE LEFT

I have become tired of being a good patient
fitting into bedsheets & procedural settings
trying to commit feeling into a state of exile
& pretending that all of life is curable

I clutch to a doctor's note
for an indecipherable thing
a list of medications that
I can't spell or pronounce
properly

I need to know what else exists

inside of this realm of illness

what happens when I don't berate

myself into productivity & standards that I can't fit into—

when irony is undone from its cruelty

& all the things we've separated show themselves as not separate

at all

& nuance becomes human

& human becomes human

I was born with 15 feet of guts
just enough room to pace
that now burns through me
holds me in a vice-grip
these things I did not know existed
till I was made to feel them

when the sublime is always in reach—
as my body is pulled back into the car seat
I am reminded that I am everything I am alive

I want to feel everything that is good
that's ugly that's distastefully mine
even in these moments that feel like the last
I am reminded that I am alive

these symptoms are my living proof
of a person distilled by a brutal world
to make a pain as primal & real

& I will feel & I will feel & I will feel
till I have used up the guts I have left
& all that remains is a love of life itself

till
each
piece
of me
has
been
pulled
apart,
till
I've
taken
every
pill,
till
I've
given
each
drop
of
blood,
till
there
is
nothing
left
to
give.

TINY WORLD

my world grew when you told me
to tune out the radio, listen to the fuzz
because it in that noise are microwaves
left over from the big bang (yes, that one)
all floating about in space, not really feeling
time at all   & it ruptures me
seeing the world through your eyes
& the things that I thought I knew
explode into new life.

INNER BABY WORK

I've taken to being the baby
in my own life — first as grown
& then as forgivably small

my partner cradles me in strong & caring arms
& places her hands on the inside of my thigh—

when the imprints of gripping hands
taunt my skins memory—
it's her hands I will think of

VITALS

holding onto the crux of feeling
we gather by the foot of the bed
to hold a séance for the living—
praying & manifesting a sign

break into a sweat   the pulse
to start or a sudden rise of the
diaphragm

ON BEING CONTAGIOUS

1.
it started in the hospital room
after the door had been closed
& the nurse had donned her plastic outfit

        'obviously'
she says
        'you're not
        but we have to
        take precautions'

it's not the first time I was made to feel
unclean—

I found out afterwards of how
my mum cried outside the door

we had both cried alone

then at some point the door opened

        & stayed that way
     there's a diagnosis
paperwork to do

& everyone could forget about it

2.

I quit my first job because I couldn't keep up
when I explained how I was just too sick
my boss crossed her arms

> 'I wouldn't have
> hired you
> if I had known'

on bank holidays working overtime
I made double the tips because I don't lie
when people ask me if I'm tired or if the day
is too long   I would've told them this too

I'm glad they got shut down in the end

I can't help my immune system

I try to contain myself

> 'you could have gotten
> all the customers sick'

s-s-s-sick

you couldn't catch me if you tried

3.

& they have tried
in school   a girl said that
I had lost so much weight
she wishes she were me—
I want to tell her
to go fuck herself
but the desire to be skinny
is punishment enough

4.

years later I get desperate
in an interview for a terrible job
that when I'm asked for a doctor's
note to prove my chronic illness
is non-contagious I just nod

at the surgery the GP looks at me
& asks me to repeat the question—
we both know it's wrong
but I can't get through the month
without it

5.

in the next prerequisite   an online form
I need to list out each of the tablets I take
& why there's a section on ways
I've hurt myself when & whether
I'd walk myself off the roof out of spite—
everyone needs insurance on me
but I cannot keep doing this

Please note Lucy suffers from a condition called ulcerative colitis. This condition can cause abdominal pain, nausea, diarrhoea, vomiting, but this is not a contagious condition.

SELF-SURGERY

when I finally give in to the fantasy
of self-surgery on the bathroom floor
with a paring knife & a flask of gin

I'll cut myself open but won't feel
a thing   all my emotions will
counteract one another   I'll

be in the comfortable anaesthesia
of adrenaline it'll start with a slice
of the skin from the ribs to pelvis

carving to find hidden mechanisms
that will be unrecognisable to me
but in my display of bloodshed

after the queasy have fainted
the rest will find themselves
in my organs—

I'll spill out pints of recycled air &
germs I have collected like a magpie
put my fingers into the wound

& trace out the different systems
steadying my trembling hands from
gritted teeth & tears my backstreet

operation is too good to stop now
the curiosity has been killing me
but I won't be prepared for the sight

of my liver teeming with alcohol
from first dates & the stuff of life
gushing to my bleeding liberal heart

I follow muscle to bone
god I feel it   I feel it now
the fantasy catches up on me

I'll have made such a mess on the floor
& be quickly out of my depth
heart pounding hard   it's a

much stronger muscle than the brain
which by then will be a thick pink
slab   all linked together by nerves

running like ants till the muscles waste
but I know that when it's my time
I'll return as something else entirely

AN EROTIC POEM FOR VAMPIRES

the intravenous line is pierced
through the back of each hand
my thin blue veins turn to wine
& speaks to me as stigmata
I can only hold out for so long
before the wound must heal—
cuts pull inwards by their edges
making the moment elusive &
fleeting from the first scratch
a vial suckles the soft pink cannula
drinking teaspoons of liquid gold
that stream out like a magician
pulling ribbons out from his sleeve
the needle moves closer to the bone
as two doctors clench at my arm
to squeeze out what I have left
when the line is placed in the nook
that sits between my upper & forearm
it starts to bruise in a purple hue
from the pushing of corticosteroids
when it is taken from a finger prick
the sting of the massage at the tips
makes me queasy & faint
as it domes it paints beds of nails
under which collects blood & flesh
from prying into myself & into
strangers I found on the internet—
from a superficial tear or an

opening without penetration
staining bedsheets & underwear
or when on the morning after
the pressure has built up in my head
enough to burst out from my nose
moving unregulated down my chin
spilling to the point of anaemia

ACKNOWLEDGEMENTS

'High Risk / High Reward' has appeared in *Ergi Press zine*. 'Astral Projection' has appeared in *Oxford Poetry*, under the title 'Disconnect'. 'Hard Times' has appeared in *Wordgathering Journal*. 'Self-Surgery' has appeared in *Isele Magazine*. 'Hard Times' and 'Self-Surgery' appear in musical compositions by Ewan East (forthcoming). 'Indigestible' was inspired by Betty Doyle and Plath. Gut Feeling references *Love Minus Love* by Wayne Holloway-Smith.

The found texts within 'Extremely Clinically Vulnerable' were taken from letter communication with the NHS in 2020 (first two passages) and Department of Health & Social Care and Ministry of Housing, Communities & Local Government in 2020 (third to fifth passages). The found text within 'On Being Contagious' was taken from a letter I had to ask my GP write in 2018.

Firstly, I would like to thank Kit Ingram and Aaron Kent at Broken Sleep for your valuable feedback and for all your hard work making this book into a reality.

Many thanks to the Creative Writing and English Department at York St John University, especially those who taught me over the years and have given feedback at various stages in this process. I am grateful to have been taught by such considerate and talented writers.

Thanks to my supervisory team, Abi Curtis, Caleb Klaces, and Rebecca Tamás, for your kindness, dedication, patience, and expertise. I am deeply grateful of how much you have pushed my work to be at its best, and for your belief in me.

A huge thanks to my family for encouraging me, looking after me, and always being there in times of need. I'm grateful for your generosity and understanding; I could not have done this without you.

Finally, thank you to Charlotte, Jeremy, Aimee, Rose, and Rachel. For your endless support, your editing skills, and for inspiring poems—thank you for love worth writing about.

LAY OUT YOUR UNREST